HALDOR LILLENAS

The Marvelous Music Maker

by

Elaine Cunningham

Beacon Hill Press of Kansas City
Kansas City, Missouri

ISBN: 083-411-4437

Printed in the
United States of America

10 9 8 7 6 5 4 3 2 1

Contents

Haldor Lillenas (1885-1959)

1

The New Baby

"Waa-aa-aa!"

"What's that?" cried John.

"I don't know," said Paul. "Sounds like a baby crying."

The two boys pushed back the quilt in their upstairs bedroom in the rough farmhouse on the island of Stord, off the coast of Norway.

The sound continued.

"Mama must have had her new baby," Paul said. "Let's find out." He stuck one toe out, touching the cold floor. "Yowee, it's cold. Get out of bed, sleepyhead," he shouted, pulling the quilt off his brother.

John jumped off the bed and ran to the window. He scraped the frost from a corner of the windowpane and looked out. Snow covered the ground. Black rocks and dark fir trees stood out like blemishes on the white surface. Far in the distance he caught a glimpse of the sea, its cold gray fingers winding in and out of the fjords (FEE-ords), the narrow inlets that cut through the cliffs near Bergen (BEAR-gen).

"There's a buggy parked in front of the house," John whispered. "Somebody's here."

Paul ran to look over his brother's shoulder. "It looks like the doctor's horse and buggy."

The two boys put on their homespun trousers and shirts and woolen socks and raced down the stairs straight into their father's arms.

"Sh-sh. Be quiet, boys, you have a new baby brother." Papa Lillenas (LIL-luh-ness) hugged his two older sons. "We will remember this day. November 19, 1885. It's little Haldor's birthday."

"Can we see him?" Paul asked.

"If you are very quiet, you may come in the bedroom and see your mama and your little brother."

As the boys tiptoed into the bedroom, a tall man with a reddish gold mustache came out. "Hello, boys, I'm Dr. Johnson. You have a beautiful baby brother. And your mother is doing fine."

The two boys looked at Mama lying on her bed. Cuddled in her arms was a tiny red-faced baby with a tuft of blond hair sticking up on top of his head.

"He's awful little," John said.

"Come closer and see him. He's a special gift from God."

Mama laid the baby on the bed beside her and held out her arms toward her bigger boys. She took hold of John and Paul's hands and carefully placed them on top of the baby's head. "Feel how soft his hair is. His skin is red and wrinkly now, but soon it will be smooth like yours."

In a few weeks life was back to normal in the Lillenas household. Papa fed the cows and did his best to feed the family. Each day became harder and harder for the family. "We must find a better place to farm," Papa said. "This 15-acre farm is hopeless. Nothing but rocks and more rocks."

"What can we do?" Mama asked. "We have three hungry boys to feed. There aren't any potatoes left to make the *lefse* (LEF-sa), and the dried *lutefisk* (LOOT-eh-fisk) is all gone."

"Remember my brother's letter that told about the wonderful land in America. Maybe we should go there." Papa stared out the window, as if looking far across the ocean.

O. P. Lillenas, Haldor's father

"America! Oh, Papa, that is so far away. Do you really think we should move to America?"

"I am seriously thinking about it." Papa turned and pounded his fist on the table. "If we could sell this farm, I would go."

"Then let's pray about it," Mama said. "If God wants us to go to America, He will send someone to buy the farm!"

2

A New Country

One day Mama and Papa gathered the three children around them in the parlor. Mama held baby Haldor, while the two older boys sat on the floor.

"We have something important to tell you, boys," said Papa. "Mr. and Mrs. Nelson have bought our farm, and I am going to America to find work."

"What about us?" John's blue eyes looked questioningly at his father.

"You three boys will stay in Fitja (FEET-yah) with Mama until I can earn enough money to send for you." Papa laid his big hands on top of John's head. "We've rented a small cabin where you will be snug and warm until you come to America."

Finally, a year later, the time came for Mama and the boys to travel to America. Mama received the money from Papa to pay the fare. Mama and the three children boarded a boat at Bergen and sailed across the stormy North Sea to England. From Liverpool they embarked on a combination passenger and cattle boat to Quebec.

From Quebec the family traveled by train to Chicago, and on to Colton, South Dakota. Papa waited for them there.

"There he is! There's Papa," shouted Paul, as the train neared the station. Both John and Paul rushed down the aisle, waiting eagerly for the conductor to let them off. Mama led Haldor by his hand, then picked him up and rushed to Papa. Tears ran down Papa's cheeks as he hugged his family again. "Praise God, we're together again," he said. "It's been a long, lonely year."

Papa helped Mama and Haldor into the buggy seat while the older boys climbed over the side themselves. Flicking his whip lightly over the back of the mare, Papa drove his family through the little town of Colton. Following a path lined with colorful flowers, waving grass, and an occasional cotton-wood tree, he brought his family to the home-stead.

The little house that Papa built stood by itself in the middle of a vast plain of prairie grass. Since there were few trees on the prairie, he had built the house with sod. He plowed a long furrow, then cut the sod into strips three feet long with a shovel. He laid the chunks lengthwise, building them up like huge bricks, to make the walls. Then he cut poles to make the roof. With branches laid on crosswise, he laid sod chunks on that. The completed house was warm and cozy in winter, and cool in summer.

Yellow grass and orange and purple flowers colored the landscape surrounding the house, and as far as you could see, there was nothing but grass and sky. Looking up at the cloudless sky, Haldor watched a bird skimming in circles. Papa saw his youngest child staring at the sky. "That's a hawk, Haldor," he said. "He's looking for a rabbit, or a mouse, for his supper." Suddenly the hawk plunged.

"There, he got something." Papa looked at Mama. "Everyone is hungry today! We should go inside and see what we can prepare for our supper."

Mama and the boys stooped down and entered the sod house. It was dark and musty inside, with hard dirt floors. Mama tried to smile. "It's very nice," she said. She walked toward the window where an animal hide flapped in the breeze.

"I even made the furniture," Papa said. Mama looked at the bed. It was made of two straight poles, nailed together for a frame, with a few more pieces nailed crosswise to form the bottom of the bed. Poles at each end for the headboard and footboard made it almost look like the bed they had left behind in Norway.

Little Haldor climbed on the mattress and jumped up and down. "We call it a straw tick," Papa said. "I made a big sack out of flour bags, then filled it with fresh straw." Haldor felt the rough straw through the cloth cover of the mattress. It felt prickly against his skin. He rolled around on the bed, then climbed down to the dirt floor.

"I can't believe how that boy has grown," Papa said. "He was a tiny baby when I left, and now he's running all over the place."

"I'll make a feather bed to cover the straw tick," Mama said. "As soon as I can get some goose feathers." She looked around the one-room shanty. "We brought quilts from Norway, and I'll hang one up to make some privacy for dressing."

"Oh, I'm glad you're here," Papa said. "Thank God, you had a safe trip, and we are here in America together."

"Do we have any neighbors?" Mama opened the leather-hinged door. "I don't see any houses nearby."

"The Johnsons live over beyond that ridge. They're Norwegian too," Papa said, pointing toward the south. "There's a little church up on the hill." He put his arm around Mama. "Most of the people here in Colton are from Norway and speak Norwegian, but we're Americans now. We'll learn to speak English."

3

Life on the Prairie

One evening, a few weeks after their arrival in South Dakota, Haldor followed his big brothers to the well behind the house. John was pulling the rope, bringing up a bucket of water, when wolves began howling not far away. "Let's get out of here," John yelled, dropping the rope. Paul ran with him, racing toward the house. Haldor tried to keep up with his brothers, but they were already at the house, leaving him alone in the dark. The wolves howled again. Closer this time. The scary sound continued. With his heart pounding in alarm, his body tense with fear, Haldor ran faster and faster, his little legs pumping up and down. He reached the house as Mama looked out the door to see where he was. She reached down and picked him up.

"Don't be scared. It's all right. There, there." She patted his back and turned toward the older boys. "You should have waited for your little brother. He's shaking like a leaf."

John and Paul started to work the next day. When they came home that night, they excitedly shared their news with Papa and Mama and Haldor. "We earned 25 cents today," said Paul.

"It was fun," added John. "We watched Mr. Johnson's cattle out in the fields and kept them from getting away."

Haldor listened to his brothers. "Mama, can we go see the cows?" he asked.

"Someday we'll walk out and visit your brothers in the fields," Mama promised.

One day Mama took Haldor, and they walked toward Mr. Johnson's fields. Blackie, a stray dog that had adopted their family, trailed at their heels. Haldor looked at the sky. A strange smell filled the air, and the sky was dark. "What is it, Mama?"

"I'm afraid it's a prairie fire." Mama looked worried. "I hope the boys are all right. Let's hurry and find them."

Mama and Haldor ran. As they came near the Johnson property, they saw flames shooting through the tall grass. Mice and rabbits ran across the path, scurrying away from the line of fire. "God, help us!" Mama prayed. "We must find those boys."

Finally, they came to the edge of the field. Haldor saw his brothers herding the cattle toward Mr. Johnson's sod shanty. "Look, Mama, there they are."

Flames leaped through the tall grass in the distance. Smoke billowed. Near the Johnson's soddie they saw Mr. Johnson frantically plowing a furrow around the house. The hot wind blew sparks over the bare strips as the cattle nervously milled around inside the furrow.

"Come quickly, boys, run," Mama yelled. Paul and John raced toward Mama and Haldor. "We must hurry home and see if our house is all right," Mama said.

The four of them ran down the path, away from the fire and smoke. "I hope the Johnsons can save their house," Mama said. As they neared their property, they saw Papa plowing a firebreak around their sod shanty. Mama led the children inside and gathered them around her. She looked at John's and Paul's smoke-darkened faces. "Thank You, Lord, for sparing our boys. Please help the Johnsons, and all of us," she prayed.

God did keep the Lillenas family safe. Their home was not burned. The Johnsons didn't fare as well. They escaped with their lives but lost their sod house and many of the cattle.

Soon after the prairie fire, Papa got sick; then John, then Haldor and Paul. "It's typhoid fever," the doctor said. "Your well water must be bad."

Mama was the only one who didn't get sick. Night and day she nursed her family. She prayed and waited on them as they lay sick in bed. For a while it looked as though they might die, but after several weeks they started to feel better.

One Sunday, after the family recovered, Mama dressed Haldor in his starched white shirt and black trousers. He went with his family to the little white church on the hill. Papa and Mama gave thanks to God for once again sparing their family.

One morning Papa told Haldor that he had a new baby sister. The baby girl was named Katrine. Haldor loved his new sister. He felt her fuzzy blond hair.

Papa sighed. "Six mouths to feed now. And we are as poor as we were in Norway."

Mama looked at him. "Are you thinking we should move again?"

"I must find work someplace. There isn't any here."

He reached up to the shelf and brought down a letter. "Listen to this. It's from my brother, Andrew." He began to read. "Doesn't it sound a lot like Norway?"

"It does," said Mama. "The way he describes the mountains, the trees, the rivers, and the ocean in Oregon makes me homesick for Norway. Let's pray about it. Maybe God will open a way for us to go west."

4

The Move West

"We've sold the farm," Papa announced one morning at breakfast.

"Does that mean we get to move to Oregon?" Paul asked.

Four-year-old Haldor looked up from the floor where he sat playing with the dog. "What about Blackie?" He hugged the dog. "Can Blackie go with us?"

"No, I'm afraid Blackie can't go on the train." Papa picked up Haldor and put him on his lap. "We'll be traveling for days, halfway across the United States." He hugged Haldor. "When we get to Kalama, Washington, we'll get on a river boat and travel on the Columbia River to Astoria, Oregon."

"But, what about Blackie?"

"We've found a good home for Blackie," Papa said. "The Johnsons have agreed to take him."

Finally the day came when Haldor and his brothers said good-bye to Blackie and to their friends. Mama carried little Katrine. Papa carried a big basket of food to eat on the way, and a large suitcase filled with clothing. Everything else was packed in a large trunk. Mr. Johnson brought his wagon and took the Lillenas family and their belongings to the Northern Pacific Railway station to begin the long trip west.

Haldor sat next to the window, beside Mama and Katrine. As the miles went by, he watched blue sky, fluffy white clouds, and waving fields of grass whiz past the window. Sometimes he saw a town, and he waved to the people at the depot. At night he curled up in his seat and slept. One day the train stopped at a station. Paul got off and came back, carrying a strange-looking object.

"Here, Haldor," he said. "Try this." Haldor looked at the long yellow fruit in Paul's hand.

"What is it?"

"It's a banana," Paul said. "I had one, and it's sweet. Try it."

Paul showed him how to peel the banana. Haldor took a bite. It tasted good. He took another bite, and another. It tasted better than anything he had ever eaten.

As the train went west, Haldor saw the land change. Pine trees covered the hills. Farther along, mountains towered above and around him. Finally, the train tracks went along a big river. "Look, Mama," he cried, staring out the window. "Look at the water."

"That's the Columbia River, Haldor. You'll see a lot of it in the days ahead."

On the fifth day after leaving South Dakota, the train chugged into the little town of Kalama, Washington. On one side of the tracks was the mighty Columbia River, on the other a small town built on a hillside.

Haldor looked around as he stepped off the train. The huge logs stacked in piles looked like mountains. "Why are there so many logs here?" he asked Papa.

"This is a sawmill," Papa said. "Men cut the trees down in the forests, then they float the logs down the river to the sawmill and stack them in these big piles." Papa lifted Haldor up so that he could see better. "Other men will cut the trees into boards to build houses and barns and stores."

Haldor had never seen so many trees in his life. He looked at the logs, then he looked at the hillsides covered with trees. It was sure different from South Dakota. He began to hum a melody, and in his mind he put words to a song about trees and mountains and rivers.

"Come, children," Mama said. "Help carry our things. We must find a place to stay."

Later, when the family had found lodging, Haldor decided to explore. After wandering around outside, he climbed the steep stairs leading to the back porch of the house and promptly fell to the bottom. Papa heard Haldor's cry and came to help him. "Supper's ready, Haldor," he said, as he carried the sobbing boy into the house. Haldor's cries ended when he saw a dish of sliced bananas on the table. For the second time in his life he had a taste of the new fruit.

When morning came, the Lillenas family boarded the stern-wheeler *The Telephone.* They settled down for the 80-mile river trip to Astoria.

Haldor, sitting beside Papa, heard a beautiful whistling, chirping sound. "What's that?" he asked.

"Why don't you find out?" Papa said. "John will go with you."

John and Haldor walked into the dining area of the boat. There, hanging in a cage, was a canary singing its beautiful song. Haldor listened to the bird as it trilled and chirped and sang.

"Let's go, Haldor," John said, after several minutes passed. "Let's go explore the rest of the boat."

"Please let me stay here," Haldor pleaded. "I want to hear the bird. It sings so pretty."

"All right," John said. "You stay right here, and I'll come back to get you."

Haldor sat on a bench and sang with the canary. In a short while, John came back. "We're heading for shore," he shouted. "We're almost to Astoria."

5

Astoria

John and Haldor rushed to the boat's rail. Papa, Mama, Paul, and Katrine stood silently watching the approaching shoreline. Haldor grabbed Papa's hand and stared across the water. Closer and closer the boat came to the town.

Astoria, Oregon, as it appeared when Haldor and his family moved there in the late 1800s.

Haldor saw huge wooden platforms resting on wooden piles driven into the tideland of the river. On top of the platforms were buildings—big buildings, small buildings, houses, stores, and fish canneries. More houses, and many trees, dotted the steep hills beyond the shoreline.

"Where will we live, Papa?" whispered Haldor.

"God will provide a place for us," Papa said. "Look, there's a sea gull landing on that post right beside the dock." Haldor watched as more gulls swarmed around the boat. Now the boat was next to the dock, and people were walking across a gangplank, leaving the riverboat.

The Lillenas family gathered their belongings together and joined the travelers. Haldor stepped onto the wooden dock. When he looked down, he could see water through the cracks. He sniffed the air. Something smelled different here. Mama looked at her small son. "Can you smell the salt water and fish?" she asked. "This is much like Norway."

Haldor looked up and saw a man running toward them. "It's your uncle Andrew," Papa said, as he threw his arms around his brother.

"Just yesterday I got your letter saying you were coming," Andrew said. "So I came to town today, and here you are. What good timing."

Uncle Andrew introduced himself to each of the family, then he led them down the street. "I imagine you're hungry," he said.

Papa looked at Mama. Neither said anything, but Paul spoke up. "Our sandwiches ran out two days ago."

"Well, well, we'll fix that. There's a good Norwegian inn here."

Haldor sniffed the air as he came into the building. It smelled like lutefisk. There was no mistaking the odor of boiled fish. After the family had eaten their fill of lefse and lutefisk, they walked around town, looking at the buildings. How strange to be walking on wooden streets with water below. The entire business section was built on platforms above the river. Looking out toward the river, Haldor saw big ships arriving from the west. He pointed at one moving slowly up the river. "Where is the boat going, Papa?"

"Those ships go on to Portland, carrying all sorts of goods to the cities upriver."

"Let's look for a house, Papa." Mama's voice had a worried sound to it. "It's starting to rain, and we need to get our belongings in somewhere."

The Lillenas family went from house to house, inquiring about a place to rent. Finally, one man said, "We have a two-room apartment below us. You may rent it if you like."

He led them down the stairs to a separate entrance below the street. "It's awfully close to the river," Mama said. "Does the water ever get inside?"

"It's high tide now," the man said. "The ocean tides come into the river here, but this is as near as it comes." River water oozed to within three feet of the door. A rotten fishy smell filled the air. "I don't know," Mama said. "What do you think, Papa?"

"I think we better take it. It's better than sleeping on the street tonight."

So the family moved their meager belongings into the two rooms under the wooden street beside the river. Their front door faced the water. Tall wooden pilings, supporting the street above, towered on either side of the door. Mama and Papa and baby Katrine slept in the combination kitchen and parlor. The three boys slept on mats in the small room behind the parlor.

Before long, Papa got a job in a sawmill. He worked 10 hours for $1.50 a day. Each day Haldor played along the river shore with his brothers. Shortly after they moved into the apartment, he heard a wonderful sound above. Notes of music ran up and down the scale. "What's that?" he asked.

"It sounds like a piano," Mama said. "The landlord must have a piano."

"Can we see it?" Haldor asked. He remembered the canary's song on the boat. He longed to hear more music.

One day Mama took Haldor and Katrine upstairs while the older children went to the store with Papa.

Timidly, she knocked on the door. "Could we look at your piano? My boy here," she pointed to Haldor, "wants to hear you play."

"Why, yes, come in." The lady took them into her parlor. There stood a tall, upright piano, the first Haldor had seen. He couldn't believe his eyes. Shiny dark brown wood glistened in the light from the window. Black and white keys lined the front of the instrument. A round stool sat in front of the piano. Three shiny pedals underneath the keyboard caught his eye.

"Would you like to hear me play?" The lady spoke both Norwegian and English, so Haldor understood what she said.

Haldor smiled. Too shy to say anything in Norwegian, let alone in English, he nodded his head.

The lady went to the stool, twirled it around a few times to adjust the height, and sat down. Haldor watched carefully. She picked up a songbook from the rack above the keyboard and opened it to a page near the front of the book. Soon he heard the most wonderful sounds. The lady's hands flew up and down the keyboard. Melodies poured forth. Thrilled, Haldor listened. "Someday I'll play a piano," he said to himself.

The door opened, and Billy came in. Haldor moved closer to Mama. Billy was the landlady's son. He was a mean boy who delighted in picking on Haldor whenever Paul and John were gone. Mama took Haldor's hand and carried Katrine toward the door. "Thank you very much for playing for us. It was lovely," she said. Mama knew how much Haldor loved music. "Maybe we could hear you play again."

"Yes, come again," the landlady said. "I'll play for you again sometime."

6

Home in the Forest

One day Papa came home and announced that he and his brother, Andrew, were going to build a house in the forest, 13 miles from Astoria.

The two men traveled in a rowboat past Smith's Point and into the beautiful Young's River. They rowed upstream two miles until they entered the Walluski River. Then they disembarked at The Landing, where the logging trains unloaded their huge logs. The logs were dumped in the stream, and they floated to the sawmills in Astoria.

The men worked hard, day after day. Haldor could hardly wait to see their new house. Paul and John had gone with Papa to help several times, but Haldor had to stay home with Mama and Katrine. One day Mama said, "Would you like to help me make lefse today?"

"Yes, yes, yes." Haldor liked to help his mother cook. First, he carefully polished the stovetop with newspaper. Then he mixed the mashed potatoes and flour until the dough was stiff.

Mama showed him how to roll the dough in a circle on the table. She helped Haldor put the circle of dough on the stovetop. After a few minutes Mama flipped it over, using a long stick. Brown spots, like freckles, appeared on the lefse. Mama flipped it over. Now there were freckles on both sides. When it was done, she folded it in half and put it in a dish towel. Later she let Haldor spread butter on the lefse and sprinkle it with sugar. Then she rolled it up, and Haldor cut it into inch-long logs.

When Papa returned to the two-room apartment in Astoria, he described the building progress. "We cut down huge trees," he said. "Sitka spruce, Douglas fir, hemlocks, and cedar." Papa took a piece of lefse and popped it into his mouth. "Some of the trees were 12 feet across at the base, and we couldn't cut them with our saw."

"What did you use?" Mama asked.

"We burned them," Papa said. "First, we drilled a large hole, then a smaller hole to meet the first one. Then we dropped red-hot coals into the large hole." Papa stopped to take another bite of the lefse. "We used hand bellows to make a strong draft to keep the flame going. The coals began to burn the tree, and after several days we had the inside burned out as large as a good-sized room."

Haldor looked around the apartment. He tried to imagine being inside a tree as big as the room. He listened carefully as Papa continued.

"The fire kept burning, until finally, with a terrific roar, the tree fell to the ground, shaking the earth when it hit."

"Then we sawed the tree into boards. We're making shingles for the roof out of logs."

Papa took another piece of lefse and swallowed it with a gulp of coffee. "*Tak for maten* (tock for MAH-ten)—thanks for the food," he said. "Let's go to bed now. I'm tired as an old bear in winter."

Finally the big day came. Time to move. Papa helped his family into the same rowboat that he and his brother had used. They took a few belongings and headed out into the Columbia River, around Smith's Point, into the Young's River, and then the Walluski. Fortunately for the family, the little logging train was at The Landing, and they were able to get transportation two miles farther up the valley to the logging camp.

"Would you like to ride up in the cab?" the engineer asked Haldor. Haldor agreed, and while the rest of the family rode on the flatcars, he "helped" the engineer drive the train as it chugged through the forest.

Arriving at the logging camp, they walked the rest of the way to the home of Simon Westbostad, who would be their nearest neighbor. Mr. Westbostad picked up Haldor and carried the tired boy into his house. The Lillenas family stayed with the Westbostads for two weeks while their little cabin, two miles farther up the deep forest, was being completed.

At the end of two weeks, Mother took Haldor by the hand and led him up the beautiful trail to their new home. Mrs. Westbostad had offered to keep Katrine until the family was settled. Haldor and Mama climbed over huge decayed trees, using the ladder that Papa had erected on both sides of the log. Through tangled brush and uneven terrain the two traveled that beautiful day. They went slowly. Mother kept knitting as they walked over the difficult path. She used every minute to make clothing for her growing family.

Haldor looked up at the huge trees, their

The Lillenas house, near Astoria, Oregon, 1890

mighty branches flowing with long, mossy streamers. He reached up to touch the silky moss. A squirrel chattered and scampered around the tree trunk. Bright blue jays scolded as Haldor and his mother approached. Several times Mama and Haldor came to rushing streams. Haldor carefully stepped across the log that Papa had placed for their use. Haldor looked at the clear water below. It seemed to sing a melody as it flowed between the brush-covered banks, dashing from rock to rock.

Finally, they saw in the distance the little house in the woods. Haldor ran ahead to where Papa and his older brothers waited.

"Welcome to your new home!" Papa shouted.

Haldor looked at the house. It stood on a foundation of heavy cedar posts, with handmade split cedar siding and a cedar shake roof. The little Walluski Creek sang its way past the house and lost itself in the deep shadows of the forest.

Haldor walked through a tangle of underbrush and ferns, and into the house. It smelled new. A few wood shavings stood in one corner, but Haldor noticed the muddy tracks covering the floor. Someone forgot to wipe his feet. A ladder went from the middle of the main room to the upstairs loft. Haldor headed for the ladder. "Is this where we sleep?" he asked.

"You and your brothers will sleep in the loft," Papa said. "Mama and I and Katrine will be downstairs."

Haldor climbed the ladder leading to the loft and looked around. The roof came down on either side, with just enough room for a boy to stand upright in the middle. Papa had piled straw under the eaves on either side. Blankets covered the straw. Haldor could hardly wait for night to come so that he could lie down on the fresh-smelling straw.

When Haldor climbed down the ladder, he heard Mama admiring the handmade furniture that Papa and Uncle Andrew had created out of fir and spruce logs. Then Mama looked in the kitchen. "How did you ever get a wood stove here?" she asked.

"We carried it the five miles from the logging camp," said Papa. "I had help, but it was really a backbreaking job." He put his arm around Mama's shoulders. "You will like it here, Mama. We have Norwegian neighbors, and they are hard workers."

One day, sometime after arriving at the new house, Mama said, "Haldor, you must learn to read. You are six years old now. I'm going to start teaching you tomorrow."

7

School Days

"I begynnelsen skapte Gud himmelen og jorden (E be-YEN-el-son SKAHP-tay Goot HIM-el-en O YOR-den). In the beginning God created the heaven and the earth." "Look, Mama, I can read the first words in the Bible." Haldor pointed to the words as he read from *Forste Mosebok* (FIR-stay MO-se-book), first book of Moses, Genesis, chapter 1, verse 1, in the Norwegian Bible.

Mama smiled at her eager son. For several months she had worked with Haldor, the first thing each morning, using the Bible as a textbook.

This morning Haldor woke early as usual, smelling coffee perking on the wood stove below. After a breakfast of freshly baked bread and coffee, Mama and Haldor went outside under the big maple tree beside the house. While Katrine slept, they sat among the ferns that rustled in the breeze at their feet. The morning was a bit chilly, but it warmed up as soon as the sun peeked over the hill.

Haldor looked at the tree-covered slopes beyond the barn that Papa had built. There was much beauty all around. And to think that God created it all. "Let's sing that song you taught me, Mama," he said.

"You mean, 'Beneath the Cross of Jesus'?"

"Yes," Haldor said, "that one." The two of them

sang until Katrine came toddling out of the house. Then Mama took her hand and led her back inside to be fed. Haldor walked behind the house to the hillside where he had his own secret place. There he sat, under the trees, and made up a little song of his own. He sang it over and over, enjoying the sound of the words that rhymed, and the tune that he composed.

One day Papa came in with some exciting news. Walking through the woods in a direction he hadn't gone before, he had found several families living less than three miles from his cabin. He also found a grocery store and a post office. One of the men that he met told him that a new schoolhouse was being built, and a road would be cut through the forest.

When the schoolhouse was completed, Haldor and his brothers walked through the woods to the little one-room frame building. Brightly colored flowers, mixed with the evergreens, lined the path. Hanging swirls of moss dangled from the trees as the boys walked the three miles. "Don't you dare speak Norwegian at school, Haldor," warned Paul. "You'll get laughed at."

Haldor didn't know a word of English. He wondered what he would do. He decided to keep his mouth shut and not say a word. All went well until afternoon recess when he climbed a tree to look at a robin's nest. When Haldor saw the baby robins, he couldn't help expressing his joy in a torrent of Norwegian.

Within a few days Haldor knew enough English to talk with his teacher and classmates.

One day, walking home from school, the three

boys heard the bloodcurdling scream of a mountain lion. Often they saw huge bear tracks. Once a black bear crossed their path, but it ran the other direction when it heard the boys coming through the woods. Many times they startled a deer as they came down the path. Sometimes they saw elk. Berries grew along the path.

One day during huckleberry season, Haldor and John decided to gather berries and take them to town to sell.

The boys got up early, took their buckets, and picked berries all day. The next day they picked more. Finally, they filled all the containers.

"Tomorrow we'll walk into town and sell these and have lots of money," John said.

Haldor could hardly sleep that night thinking of the trip they would take the next day. Early in the morning, he and John dressed in their best clothes. Then they slipped down the loft ladder and into the kitchen. Mama greeted them. "Good morning, boys, I'm fixing sandwiches for you to take on your hike to Astoria. Eat your breakfast while I make the sandwiches."

When the boys finished eating, they put the sandwiches in their pockets, grabbed the handles of the heavy buckets of berries, and headed toward Astoria, 13 miles away.

They walked the three miles to the village of Olney. As they trudged along, the miles grew longer, the hills higher, and the buckets heavier.

When they finally reached the business section of Astoria, they went from store to store, trying to sell their berries. Everybody had berries. No one wanted more.

Lugging the heavy buckets up over a steep hill, the boys stopped at the home of Andrew Bue, a friend of the family.

Mr. Bue saw them coming. "What do we have here?" he said.

The hot, tired boys came up on the porch. "We can't get anybody to buy our berries." Haldor began to cry.

"We walked all the way to town, and everybody has berries." John sat on the porch steps and mopped his forehead. "We don't know what to do."

"I'll tell you what," Mr. Bue said, "I think Mrs. Bue wants some berries for pies. How about if I buy them all?

"Mama," he called inside, "come and see who's here."

A short, plump lady came through the door. "Well, my, my, if it isn't the Lillenas boys. How nice to see you." She picked up a huckleberry. "What nice berries. But, you boys must be tired and hungry. I'll fix supper, and you can stay overnight."

After a night's rest, the boys took the 50 cents that Mr. Bue gave them and bought tickets to ride the steamboat back to Olney.

When they arrived home with empty buckets and empty pockets, and told their story to the family, Mama patted them on their heads. "I'm glad you are both back safe and sound. It's more important to be honest and hardworking than to get money.

"Now, come and help me clean up the house. It's our turn to have the church service here tomorrow."

8

Saying Good-bye

The nights grew colder as fall moved into winter. Maples and birch trees shed their leaves; but the evergreens stood silhouetted against empty gray sky, still wearing their dark green needles.

Excitement filled the house as Christmas approached. One day Papa said, "You boys can go with me to Astoria to shop for presents." He gave each of the boys 35 cents to spend on Christmas presents. Mama would stay home with Katrine and the new baby, George, who had recently been born.

The three boys and Papa made their way through the woods to The Landing. Haldor inhaled the clean, cold air in deep breaths. What could be more exciting than going Christmas shopping with Papa? And to have 35 cents of his very own to spend for presents was like frosting on Mama's scones. He went down the list in his mind. Mama, Papa, John, Paul, Katrine, baby George, and Uncle Andrew. Five cents to spend on each.

After a chilly trip by boat up the river, they walked from the dock to the main street of Astoria. Everywhere they went they heard the exciting news that Captain George Flavel's mansion on

Duane Street glowed with lights. Something called *electricity* provided the power. Papa and the boys walked up Duane Street and gazed in awe at the sight. On that gray December afternoon, just before Christmas, the sight of chandeliers with lights as bright as the sun, hanging from the ceiling in room after room, made a shiver of joy run up and down Haldor's back. Wouldn't it be wonderful if sometime they could have lights in their house. But Papa wasn't rich like the famous Captain Flavel, who owned ships and property.

When the 35 cents was spent, Haldor clutched his gifts in his arms and followed Papa and his brothers to the dock. By the time they reached home, it was dark. As they walked up the long lane, Haldor saw a lone candle glowing in the kitchen window of their little cabin in the woods. He could see Mama bustling around inside. A warm feeling spread through his heart. He wouldn't trade his home and family for any mansion in the world, even if it was lighted with electricity from top to bottom.

The next day was the day before Christmas. Fragrant baking smells filled the kitchen. Papa spent most of the day in the woodshed. Haldor could hear him whistling as he hammered and sawed. What could he be making?

While Mama prepared supper, Papa took the boys to the woods to find the best evergreen tree in the forest to use as their Christmas tree. Proudly carrying the little hatchet that Papa gave him, Haldor thought of the toys he had made out of scraps of wood. They were hidden in the loft so that Katrine wouldn't see them before Christmas.

They chopped the tree down, and Papa dragged it home. Each of the boys carried cedar boughs to cut into small pieces and scatter on the freshly scrubbed floors. With the tree in the center of the room, and the pungent fragrance of western cedar filling the house, you could almost imagine that you were out in the forest.

They all dressed in their best clothes for Christmas Eve. Gathered near the tree, Haldor and his brothers and sister sat quietly as Papa read the Christmas story from the Bible. Then the children joined hands and marched around the tree, singing Christmas carols.

Finally, the time came to distribute gifts. Haldor quickly climbed the ladder and brought down the wooden toys for Katrine and baby George. Then he distributed the gifts that he had bought in Astoria. Papa went to the woodshed and brought out his surprise—a brand-new sled for the boys. He also gave new shoes to each child. During the long winter days, when there were no jobs available, Papa had tanned hides to make leather. Using the cobbler's skills that he learned in Norway, Papa had made handmade shoes for everyone. Haldor was especially excited to get leather shoes. He had been wearing wooden shoes and was ashamed of them. One time, after walking two miles with his brothers to visit the neighbor's children, he had hidden behind a stump so that no one would see his wooden shoes.

One day, after Christmas, a neighbor brought a black cow into the settlement. The neighbors invited the Lillenas family to come over for milk and bread. It was a real treat to have milk. Butter, milk, eggs, and fruit were scarce in the Lillenas home. Once Mama tried to make a fruit substitute out of "sour grass" she gathered in the forest. It tasted terrible.

Conditions grew worse. In the year 1900 Papa made another startling announcement to his family. "I've sold our house and farm to Andrew for $400. We're moving to a Norwegian settlement in Paynesville, Minnesota."

Taking advantage of a special rate on the railroad, Papa bought tickets for $10.00 each for the family to travel from Portland, Oregon to St. Paul, Minnesota. Once again, they packed a few belongings and boarded a riverboat for Portland. Many friends gathered at the dock to wave goodbye. Mama, who never did learn to speak English, sang a beautiful Norwegian farewell song.

In Minnesota, Papa located an abandoned house in the country. The owner let the Lillenas family stay there the first winter. Wind blew through the cracks in the wall, and snow piled up inside the windowsills. One day, Mama caught a cold. She grew worse as the days went by. She coughed and sneezed. She looked thin and pale. "We must find another place to live," Papa said.

Finally, he located a 40-acre tract of land for $600 in Hawick, Minnesota. Here, he built a three-room house, and the boys helped clear the land. But Mama got sicker and sicker. One day the doctor said, "Mrs. Lillenas, I'm sorry to tell you this, but you have tuberculosis."

Haldor knew that tuberculosis was a serious lung disease. Mama coughed more and more. She lost weight. Haldor was 15 now and attended a Lutheran church. On the Sunday that Haldor stood in front of the church altar with the other members of his confirmation class and promised to forsake the world, the flesh, and the devil, his mother sat in the last pew, struggling to breathe, but watching with loving eyes as her son joined the church.

With each passing day Mama grew weaker until one day, in her pain, she said, "Pray that Jesus may come soon to take me home."

Haldor sat outside his mother's bedroom door, listening to her gasps for breath and her spells of coughing. Why did she have to suffer? Why did she have to be sick and die? And now John coughed and wheezed like Mama. What if both Mama and John died? Haldor tried to pray, but it seemed like his prayers bounced off the ceiling. Papa came out of the bedroom and put his arm around Haldor's shoulders. "Don't grieve, Son. Mama is ready to go. In fact, she wants to be with the Lord." His voice broke, but he continued, "She'll be better off. But oh, how we'll miss her." With sagging shoulders, Papa slowly walked back into the room where his wife lay dying.

Three days later, a long line of wagons followed the wagon that carried the plain pine casket covered with wild cherry blossoms. Haldor looked at the casket, his heart breaking. Good-bye, Mama. He would miss her prayers at the dinner table and her voice singing the hymns of the church. But Haldor knew it was just his mother's worn-out body lying in the box. Mama was in heaven, probably already singing songs of praise with the angels.

9

A New Friend

"Papa, I think I'll leave home and look for a job," Haldor announced one morning as he drank a cup of coffee and ate a piece of bread for his breakfast. "It's just not the same around here with Mama gone."

Papa poured himself a cup of coffee and sat at the table. "Where do you plan to go, Son?"

"I don't know. I'll just walk down the road until I find a farmer who needs help, I guess."

"We'll miss you, Haldor, but if you feel you have to go, then I guess you better go. There's not much work here, that's for sure."

Haldor packed two flannel shirts and an extra pair of overalls in an old suitcase, made a sandwich, and headed down the country road. He stopped at farm after farm, but no one needed help. Finally, he came to a farm where they offered him a job.

"We'll pay you $8.00 a month," the farmer said. "You can sleep in the cheese factory at night."

Haldor worked hard, milking eight cows morning and evening and working in the hayfields during the hottest part of the day. At night, he flopped on a mat in the cheese factory, thankful for a place to stay, though the pungent odor of several hundred cheeses curing kept him awake each night.

After several weeks, Haldor found another job with a neighboring farmer. Here he got so homesick that he quit his job after a few days. For his pay, the farmer gave him a pair of overalls and a baby pig. Haldor put the pig over his shoulders and carried it the 15 miles home.

When Haldor arrived home, he discovered that his father and oldest brother, Paul, were making plans to homestead in western North Dakota. John sat in a chair, coughing. Haldor was alarmed to see how thin and pale his brother looked.

After everyone had greeted Haldor, Papa reached up to the top of the cupboard and brought down an envelope. "Here's a letter for you from Oregon," he said.

Haldor ripped it open. Inside was an offer of employment with one of their former neighbors in Oregon. He read the letter aloud. "I think I'll accept this," he said. "Maybe that's why I couldn't find any good job here."

A few days later, on a snowy November day, John walked with Haldor to the Great Northern depot, and Haldor said good-bye once again as he headed west. As he looked out the train window, Haldor saw his tall, fair-haired brother trudging slowly back toward the homestead. Tears came to Haldor's eyes as he realized that he would probably never see John again.

In the woods of Oregon, near his former home, Haldor worked clearing land, grubbing stumps, and doing other hard work. He received $100 for seven months.

His next job was with an old fisherman, fishing for salmon. They used a sailboat 20 feet long and 6 feet wide. With a gill net 1,500 feet long, they drifted all night, hoping to fill the net with salmon. Often they found only a small flounder or two in the net the next morning. When they weren't fishing, Haldor and the fisherman lived in an old scow on the banks of the river. Haldor's income for the four months was $20.00 a month.

While he was in Oregon, Haldor got the sad news from his father that John had died. Mr. Lillenas told how they had moved to North Dakota in a boxcar during a blizzard. The family, trapped in the storm in the boxcar with no heat, nearly froze. John, weakened by tuberculosis, soon died. "He died a Christian," Papa wrote in his letter. "John's last words were 'Everything is radiant.'"

Sitting on the bank of the Columbia River, Haldor read the letter and thought of his favorite brother, now in heaven with Mama. He wondered if he would ever see them again.

At the end of two years, Haldor headed back to North Dakota to work on his father's farm, for no salary. During the long winter months, when there was little farm work to be done, Haldor sat at the kitchen table, huddled near the kerosene lamp, studying a chemistry book that he had ordered from a correspondence course.

One day Haldor was reading a magazine and saw an advertisement that described the fortune you could make writing songs. Haldor decided then and there that he would be a songwriter.

Haldor sent his first song, "Dreaming of Days Gone By," to a Cincinnati publisher. A contract arrived in the mail. It promised heavy royalties, but with the agreement that Haldor pay part of the expense of publication. Haldor sent in the requested $25.00 but only received a total of $3.65 in royalties. Several other songs were published, but Haldor received no money for them. Haldor decided that he would never get rich writing songs.

In 1906 Haldor returned to Astoria, Oregon, and found a job in a box factory. He attended church occasionally but knew he was not a Christian.

One beautiful July evening, he walked down the street and saw a group of people standing on the corner singing gospel songs. Haldor moved closer, drawn by the music. A young woman sang a song he had never heard before: "O angels, tell my mother I'll be there." God spoke to Haldor's heart. He thought of his mother and the many prayers she had prayed for him before she died.

A young man began to speak. He told how God had saved him from a life of sin, and now he had peace in his heart. Haldor listened intently to the testimony. After the meeting, he talked to the young man. "Where are you from?" he asked.

"We meet at the Peniel Mission each week," the young man replied. "Would you like to visit our services?"

"Yes, I would," Haldor said. "What time do they start?"

"We meet every Sunday morning and evening and several nights during the week. Would you like to come with me this Sunday?"

Haldor went to the mission that Sunday. He sat on a wooden bench beside his new friend, enjoying the lively singing. After the service, he promised to come again.

The following Sunday night, at the close of the preacher's sermon, an invitation was given to come forward and pray. Haldor walked to the altar and knelt humbly at the wooden railing. The preacher knelt on the other side of the altar and opened a big black-covered Bible. It reminded Haldor of the Bible his mama used to read when she gathered the family around for family devotions.

The minister showed Haldor the verse in Romans 3:23 that said, "For all have sinned, and come short of the glory of God." Haldor knew that he was a sinner. Then the preacher pointed to 1 John 1:9, and Haldor read, "If we confess our sins, he is faithful and just to forgive us our sins." Haldor began to tell the Lord how sorry he was for his sins. He believed the Word of God and knew that he was forgiven. He became a new person in Christ Jesus.

Walking down the hilly street that evening, Haldor looked up into the sky above Astoria. Never had it looked so beautiful. A million stars blinked back at him. It seemed that the whole universe rejoiced. Haldor hummed a song and realized it was the one his mother had taught him years before, "Beneath the Cross of Jesus." Now he knew what the words meant. He was a Christian tonight because Jesus died on the Cross. Haldor felt clean and new. "This must be what it means to be born again," he said aloud. "I'm a new person."

A few nights after Haldor's conversion, he brought his best friend, Bernt Saterbo, to the mission, and Bernt also became a Christian.

Haldor faithfully attended the little mission. He

helped with the music and went out with the group, holding street meetings. Through studying his Bible and hearing it preached, Haldor learned about the Holy Spirit. One day he asked the Holy Spirit to have full control of his life from that day on.

Haldor continued to write songs, both words and music. He sent them to different publishers, but no one wanted them. Haldor kept writing. Finally a kindly hymn writer wrote some encouraging words and published one of the songs, "The Way He Leads Is Best for Me." Another song, "I Shall See Him Face-to-Face," was published, and then still another: "He Set Me Free."

He set me free, He set me free,
I was blind but hallelujah, now I see!
I shall ne'er forget the day
When He washed my sins away
And He set, He set me free.

This song became popular in camp meetings and opened the door for Haldor to do what he loved to do—write songs about his best friend, Jesus Christ.

10

The Call of God

"Shall I be a chemist or a minister?" A struggle began in Haldor's heart. He had moved to Portland, Oregon, to work in the laboratory of the Woodward Drug Company as a chemist, but day after day he felt a stronger urge to work full-time in the service of his new Master.

The year 1908 was decisive for Haldor. He joined a brand-new denomination, the Church of the Nazarene. He decided he would give up his career as a chemist to become a minister. He worked with the Peniel Mission in Portland for a year, then met J. H. James, the man in charge of the Salvation Army corps in Santa Rosa, California.

"Would you like to travel with our group, holding revival services?" Mr. James asked Haldor.

"I'm a member of the Church of the Nazarene," Haldor said.

"That's all right. You can sing and travel with us and keep your membership as a Nazarene." When Haldor seemed interested, the man said, "We'll pay you $5.00 a week and your expenses."

The Peniel Mission Group, 1906. (Haldor stands second from the left.)

So Haldor put on a Salvation Army uniform and joined a group of six men called the "Charioteers' Brigade." They held street meetings and revival services in little mining towns throughout California. Many people were converted.

A covered wagon, decorated with Scripture verses, was prepared for the men to use in their travels. A team of lively horses pulled the wagon. One hot July day, driving out of Sacramento, the driver drove the wagon under a large shade tree and removed the bridles from the horses, replacing them with feed bags.

"You better put the bridles back on," Haldor advised.

"No, they'll be all right," the driver said. "Don't worry."

The men sat down to enjoy the lunches they had brought with them. Suddenly a brisk breeze rattled the limbs of the tree, rubbing them against the top of the wagon. The frightened horses started to run away.

Immediately all six men jumped up and ran toward the horses, pushing them against a nearby barbed-wire fence to try to stop their wild flight. The horses jumped over the fence, dragging the wagon with them. Drums, guitars, banjos, horns, and wheels flew in all directions. The ruined wagon ended the travels for that day.

In 1909 Haldor heard about Deets Pacific Bible College in Los Angeles. He knew he didn't have enough money to go to college, so he prayed and asked God to show him what to do.

Rev. A. O. Hendricks, pastor of Portland Church of the Nazarene, took a special offering one Sunday, and the people gave enough money to pay Haldor's train fare to Los Angeles.

Haldor bought his ticket and packed his suitcase for college. He had $9.00 dollars in his pocket. At the depot, Mrs. Hendricks handed Haldor a cardboard box. "This is for you to have on the way to Los Angeles," she said. After Haldor boarded the train, he looked in the box and found sandwiches and cookies and bananas, enough for the whole trip.

When Haldor located the little college in Los Angeles, he registered for his classes and then went job hunting. "If I can work half-days and go to school half-days, I believe I can make it through this year," he said.

Haldor found a job working in a coal yard. The work was dirty, but it helped to pay his bills. Later in the year he became choir director at a Nazarene church in Los Angeles.

During his first year in college, Haldor wrote many songs. One of them was "Holiness Forevermore." The Holy Spirit, who filled his heart back in Oregon, still guided and directed him day by day.

11

Bertha Mae

One morning in chapel, the song leader announced that Miss Bertha Mae Wilson would sing a special song. A dark-haired, brown-eyed young lady began to sing. Her beautiful voice filled the room. Haldor sat in a daze. "I'd like to meet her," he thought. "I wonder if she would even look at me." He decided he'd find out. After chapel he waited at the door until she came out, then walked beside her to her class. "I really enjoyed your song, Miss Wilson," he said.

"Why, thank you, Haldor," she replied. "I've heard you play the piano. Would you like to play for me some time?"

"How about this afternoon when I get off work at five o'clock?"

"All right, I'll meet you in the music practice room," Bertha Mae said.

Haldor could hardly wait until five o'clock. The hours dragged by. Finally, he finished his job, cleaned up, and rushed to the practice room. Bertha Mae sat at the piano, her nimble fingers playing scales up and down the keyboard. When she saw Haldor, she got up. "I have a copy of the new song you wrote—'Holiness Forevermore.' Let's try singing it together."

Haldor was happy to find out that she had a copy of one of his songs. When they sang together, he was even more thrilled. Their voices blended beautifully. Later they, and another couple, formed a mixed quartet and sang for many churches in the area.

Bertha Mae's father pastored the Mary Street Church of the Nazarene in Pasadena. Bertha was studying to be a minister like her father.

Haldor went often to the Nazarene parsonage to visit Bertha Mae. One day, as they sat together near the piano in the parlor, they noticed a shiny spot of light flashing on the ceiling.

"What's that?" Bertha said.

"I don't know, but let's look out on the porch. It could be that rascally little brother of yours. Maybe he's up to something again."

Haldor and Bertha Mae tiptoed to the open window and carefully moved the curtain to one side. Right in front of their eyes was a cardboard tube rigged up like a periscope. A mirror near the top reflected into the room. At the bottom of the tube was a small, brown-haired boy—Mallalieu (MAL-a-lew) Wilson, Bertha's younger brother.

"What are you doing?" Bertha Mae asked.

"I just wanted to see what you two were doing in the parlor," Mallalieu replied.

"Well, you don't need to spy on us," Bertha Mae said. "We weren't doing anything wrong. Anyway, it's none of your business what we are doing."

Mallalieu jumped up and ran around the side of the house toward the barn where he liked to hide.

Before the year ended, Haldor had asked Bertha Mae to marry him. The following summer they were married in her father's church.

Haldor and his wife, Bertha Mae

Bertha Mae finished her last year of college in 1910, the year that Deets Pacific Bible College moved to a new campus in Pasadena.

One day Haldor and Bertha Mae walked beneath the palm trees in Pasadena, admiring the roses in full bloom. "What do you think about the church in Lompoc wanting us to come as its pastors?" Haldor asked.

"I believe God wants us to go there to pastor," Bertha Mae said. "It's not a very big church, but we have a big God, and He will supply our needs."

Haldor agreed. So in the fall of 1910 they moved to Lompoc, 60 miles north of Santa Barbara, 9 miles inland from the Pacific Ocean. The church members in Lompoc had rented a small, three-room parsonage for their new pastor and his wife. Haldor and Bertha Mae moved in. A loaf of home-made bread sat on the little wooden kitchen table. Beside it stood a jar of strawberry jam, a dozen eggs, and some sweet corn. Haldor put his arms around his new wife. "My dear Bertha, I don't have much to offer you financially, but I love you with all my heart." He looked at the food on the table. "And it looks like our people love us already."

Before long, Bertha Mae taught piano students, and Haldor wrote more songs. This helped their income a bit. The church paid them what came in for the offerings, usually about $3.00 per week.

One Sunday evening, as Haldor looked over his sermon for that night, he looked out the window toward the west. A beautiful sunset filled the sky. Violet clouds, streaked with pink and gray, mingled with the gold of the sun and stretched from side to side as far as he could see. Haldor opened his Bible and read in Revelation 21:23, "And the city had no need of the sun, neither of the moon, to shine in it: for the glory of God did lighten it, and the Lamb is the light thereof."

"What a wonderful song that would be," he said. "To think of a city that doesn't need the sun."

After church that night, Haldor sat down at the kitchen table and wrote the words of a song he called "Where They Need No Sun." The next day he wrote the music and mailed it to Rev. Charles Scoville, an evangelist.

"Bertha, I picked up the mail at the post office, and guess what? We've been invited to direct the music at Los Angeles First Church for the District Sunday School Convention."

"Wonderful," Bertha said. "But how can we afford to go on our little salary? The train fare alone is $25.00."

"God will provide if we trust Him," Haldor said. "I'll write and tell them we plan to come."

The weeks passed, and there was no money for the trip. Finally, on Friday, before they were to leave on Monday, Haldor counted the money on hand. They still needed $4.50 of the $25.00. That night, when they knelt to pray, both of them felt that God would supply the need. They thought perhaps the Sunday offerings would be unusually large. It was Bertha Mae's turn to preach that Sunday morning. When the service ended, the offering was handed to Haldor. He counted it, and it amounted to $1.56.

As they walked home, Haldor said, "Do you think we are going to Los Angeles tomorrow morning?"

"Oh yes," Bertha Mae replied, "there can be no doubt about that."

At the evening service, Haldor preached, and the offering was $1.16.

Neither of them doubted that God would supply. They slept well that night. The train was due to leave at nine the next morning. Eight o'clock arrived, and Haldor heard the locomotive blowing off steam, ready for the nine-mile drive to Surf, where connections were made with the Southern Pacific main line.

"Why don't you call the post office, Haldor?" Bertha Mae said. At 8:30, Haldor called the post office. There were two letters there. He rushed down the street and got the mail. The first envelope contained a telephone bill for $1.20. Haldor tore open the other. Out fell a check for $25.00 from Charles Scoville. In the letter enclosed with the check Mr. Scoville wrote that the song "Where They Need No Sun" had been adopted as his theme song for his revival meetings. Thousands of people were singing the song every night with great enthusiasm, and the check enclosed was to pay for the song and several others that Haldor had sent him.

"Praise the Lord!" Haldor said.

The postmaster looked at him. "Did you get some good news?"

"Did I ever!" Haldor beamed from ear to ear. "God just supplied the exact amount of money that we need to take a train trip in just a few minutes." With that he said good-bye and ran across the street to the bank to cash the check, then home to tell Bertha the good news. They reached the depot just in time to jump on the train for the trip to Los Angeles.

One day in Lompoc, Haldor looked into the face of his new baby daughter, who was born at five o'clock that morning. They named her Evangeline. Soon after that, Haldor enrolled in the University Extension School of Music in Chicago, taking classes by correspondence. He completed the course in three years.

During the pastorate at Lompoc, Haldor directed the music at his first camp meeting. A huge tent was erected on the campus of Pasadena Nazarene College. Thousands attended, and many hundreds accepted Christ as their Savior. Haldor, thrilled to see what God could do, determined to give his whole life to preaching and writing music to the glory of God.

12

Some Golden Daybreak

"The church in Pomona, California, has asked us to be their pastors," Haldor announced one morning when he came home from the post office. "What do you think we should do?"

"Let's pray about it and see what God shows us," Bertha Mae replied.

After praying, the young couple decided to accept the call. They moved with their baby girl and soon felt at home in the beautiful city of Pomona, surrounded by orange groves and roses.

One day, after helping in a revival meeting in Lincoln, Nebraska, Haldor came home feeling sick. "I think you better ask the doctor to come and see me," he told Bertha Mae.

When the doctor came, he said, "You only have six months to live. It looks like you have tuberculosis."

"Oh, no," Haldor said. "I can't die. I'm only 28 years old, and I have a wife and baby to support."

"I'm afraid you don't have any choice," the young doctor declared.

After much prayer, Haldor and Bertha Mae decided to store their few belongings and move to Oregon. With sad hearts, but trusting in God, they packed and cleaned and prepared to move.

Early one morning, a few days before they were to leave, Haldor stood at the kitchen window looking out over the San Gabriel Mountains toward the Mojave Desert. Mockingbirds filled the air with song. The rising sun clothed the mountains in brilliant colors. Lavender, violet, powder blue, gold, and crimson colored the sky. "I've never seen such a beautiful sunrise," Haldor said. Then he thought about dying. "But soon I'll see a daybreak far more beautiful when I get to heaven." He began to hum a tune and grabbed a piece of paper. That morning the words of "Some Golden Daybreak" were written.

Someday the light of earth shall fade away,
And I, at last, shall cease to roam;
Then burdens I have borne I down shall lay;
Some golden daybreak in my home, sweet home.

Peace came to his heart. He knew that God could heal him here on earth or take him to heaven. Either way he was the Lord's.

God chose to heal. Up in the woods of Oregon, Haldor recovered, and within a few months he moved his wife and daughter back to Pomona to pastor the church again.

As the years passed, Haldor wrote hundreds of hymns. One that was especially loved was "Wonderful Peace." In 1914 an invitation came for Haldor and Bertha Mae to be part of the Scoville Evangelistic Team, so they packed up their clothing and took their little girl and traveled from city to city, holding services nightly, helping with the music and meetings.

One day the exciting news came that Bertha Mae's father, Rev. W. C. Wilson, had been elected general superintendent at the General Assembly of the Church of the Nazarene. Before Christmas, the same year, Haldor and Bertha Mae received the sad news that her father had died. In 1916 a son, Wendell Haldor, was born. With two children, Haldor felt they should have a home of their own, so they built a three-bedroom home at Olivet, Illinois, near the Nazarene college.

One day after they moved in, Haldor said, "If we just had a piano, we could write more songs."

"Well, I saw an organ at our neighbor's house the other day," Bertha Mae said. "It sounds kind of wheezy, so she told me they would sell it for $5.00."

"Let's get it," Haldor said.

With the old organ in their parlor, Haldor wrote many songs. Among them was the music to both "It Is Glory Just to Walk with Him" and "Jesus Has Lifted Me."

In 1916 a call came to pastor the small church in Auburn, Illinois. Part of the time Bertha Mae served as pastor while Haldor traveled as a song evangelist. And always Haldor wrote songs. One year he wrote 200 songs, many of them written while he traveled from church to church holding meetings.

When Haldor came home between meetings, he told his family about the wonderful times when God's Spirit came on the services and many people found Christ as their Savior. "I'm so glad that God is using my songs to reach people's hearts, even if I don't get much money for them."

Haldor remembered when, as a child, he wrote to the magazine that said you could make a fortune writing songs. "I've never made a fortune," he said. "In fact, I only received $5.00 for one of my most popular songs."

"Which one is that?" Bertha Mae asked.

"'Wonderful Grace of Jesus,'" Haldor said. "It's being sung everywhere. I'm happy that God is using it. The money isn't important to me."

One day Haldor came home with exciting news. "I've bought a car. It's a 1915 Buick."

Haldor took his family for a ride. They had never had a car before, and Haldor drove carefully down the street, around the block, and back home. He steered the car into the garage—and then it happened. He forgot how to brake. Crash! The car slammed into the brick wall of the garage. No one was injured, but the crankshaft of the car was broken. After that, Haldor remembered to use the brakes to stop the car.

Bertha Mae had planted a flower garden behind the garage. One hot, sultry day a cloudburst came. Rain pelted the flowers to the ground. When the storm ended and the sun came out, Haldor went back to see the damage to the flowers. To his surprise, the flowers stood tall in the sunshine, blooming brightly. A rainbow hung in the sky. Haldor ran to the house for a piece of paper and wrote another beautiful song.

Like the sunshine after rain,
Like a rest that follows pain,
Like a hope returned again,
*Is the peace that Jesus gives.**

In 1919 the Lillenases resigned the church at Auburn; and after a few months of travel in revival meetings, they moved to Peniel, Texas, where they pastored for one year. During that time Haldor wrote more songs and published a hymnbook called *Special Sacred Songs.* One day, he came home with the news that the church in Redlands, California, had called them to pastor. In a short time Haldor and Bertha Mae and their children climbed into their new Model-T Ford and headed west.

13

God Will Take Care of You

"Look at the big mountains," eight-year-old Evangeline said, as her daddy drove the Ford up the highway leading to Redlands.

"Yes, Honey, and those are real oranges growing on those trees you see along the road."

The family arrived in Redlands hot and tired, but happy to be in such beautiful surroundings. The church building wasn't as beautiful. You could see through the walls, and the roof was missing.

"We don't have any money to complete our building project," said the chairman of the board one evening.

"Let's have an all-night prayer meeting," Haldor said.

The people agreed. By midnight everyone felt that God would answer their prayers. They went home and to bed.

"I dreamed that the First National Bank gave us a loan," Haldor told his wife the next morning.

"Maybe you better go see them today," she said.

Haldor went and explained the situation and came home rejoicing that God had answered prayer. He had the needed money to finish the building.

Haldor kept writing songs—hundreds more. Two of the best-known ones were "Jesus Will Walk with Me" and "Living Forever."

One night when the family was asleep in the upstairs bedrooms, Haldor heard the creaking of footsteps. He went downstairs and found the back door open and a drawer open in the kitchen. No one seemed to be around. Then he looked through the four bedrooms upstairs.

"I think I'll check the bathroom," he told Bertha Mae, "then I'll go back to bed."

Bertha Mae crept behind him as he checked the bathroom. When he went inside the room, he whispered, "There's someone in here." Bertha Mae screamed. Behind the door a huge man hid. The man ran, with Haldor right behind him. Haldor chased him down the stairs and out the door. Silverware lay scattered on the back porch. When Haldor gathered it up, he found the burglar's shoes. He had escaped so fast that he left his shoes on the steps.

The next day Haldor bought a gun. Each time the family came home from church, they checked the house, Haldor leading the way with the gun.

One day, at the dinner table, Haldor prayed, thanking God for everything. When he finished, he said, "I'm going to sell the gun. I've been thinking about the song Evangeline sang in church last Sunday, 'God Will Take Care of You,' and I really believe He will take care of us. We don't need the gun."

In the year 1923, the Lillenas family sold their furniture and said good-bye to the good people in Redlands. Once again they felt God leading them, this time to pastor Indianapolis First Church of the Nazarene. They loaded the car with a mattress, tent, camping equipment, and their two children and drove over the Cajon Pass, through the Mojave Desert, and east.

On a detour in eastern Colorado the heavily loaded car sank into a mudhole. The family was stranded. Worst of all were the buzzing clouds of mosquitoes surrounding the car. Haldor found some old rags. He struck a match and started the rags smoldering. Then he waved the smoking rags around during the night to keep the mosquitoes away so that his family could get some sleep. The next morning Haldor borrowed a shovel from a nearby farmer and dug the car out of the mud.

They arrived in Kansas City in time for the 1923 General Assembly of the church, then drove on to Indianapolis to their new pastorate.

"Oh, what a dreary-looking building," Bertha Mae said, when they saw the church building.

"And there's no parsonage," Haldor said. "We'll have to find a place to rent. But thank the Lord, we are safely here."

They finally found two furnished rooms to rent. Before long the church attendance grew to 260, a new church was built, and a new parsonage purchased.

One of the songs Haldor wrote while they were in Indianapolis was "Your Roses May Have Thorns."

"Mrs. Lillenas and I will sing a new song that

someone here may need tonight," Haldor announced one evening in church.

As they started to sing, a man walked in the door. He had just gotten out of prison. Discouraged, and ready to give up, he had been walking down the street and saw the lighted Church of the Nazarene. It was filled with people singing and seeming to have a good time. He decided to go inside and sat down as the Lillenases stood to sing.

Haldor and Bertha Mae sang, "Your roses may have thorns, but don't forget your thorns may have some roses too." God spoke directly to the man's heart, and he later testified that he was a changed man, ready to live for God. "Victory came to me on the wings of a song," he said.

After three happy years pastoring in Indianapolis, Haldor decided to work full-time writing and publishing music. He organized the Lillenas Publishing Company. Besides writing and selling music, Haldor traveled as an evangelist.

One cold, dreary day in November of 1928, Haldor was traveling toward Pittsburgh in his 1923 Buick. He missed his family and wished he was home. Reaching the outskirts of the city, he noticed that the smog was so bad that he had to turn on the car lights.

At four o'clock he finally located the Church of the Nazarene where he was to hold a convention. No one was there, but the building was open. Haldor entered the dimly lit building. He went to the basement and looked through the classrooms. In one he discovered a small organ. He got a chair and sat down to play, feeling a deep sense of loneliness.

As he played, words and music of a new song came to him:

How can I be lonely
When I've Jesus only
To be my Companion and unfailing Guide?
Why should I be weary,
Or my path seem dreary,
*When He's walking by my side?**

A great sense of peace and the nearness of the Lord filled the room. Haldor knew he would never be alone. Jesus walked by his side.

In 1930 the Lillenas Publishing Company business was sold to the Nazarene Publishing House of Kansas City, Missouri. Haldor moved his family to Kansas City to become manager of the music department of Nazarene Publishing House. The music department began printing and selling music under the name Lillenas Publishing Company.

Glorious Gospel Hymns, published by the Lillenas Publishing Company at Nazarene Publishing House, became the official hymnal of the Church of the Nazarene in early 1931. It contained 72 hymns with words and music written by Haldor Lillenas, and 20 other songs for which he composed the tune only.

Everything looked great for Haldor, but a dark shadow entered his life. Bertha Mae was not well.

*Copyright 1928. Renewed 1955 by Lillenas Publishing Co.

14

Melody Lane

Haldor felt sad. He hated to leave the house that morning because his wife was so sick. Later, as he drove down Paseo Boulevard on his way to his office, he thought of happier days when the children were home and he and his wife took turns preaching in church. Now the outlook seemed as dismal as the gray, foggy day. Though Bertha Mae still tried to write songs, he knew that she was very ill. Haldor felt discouraged.

Suddenly, it seemed that Someone was in the car, sitting on the seat beside him. Haldor felt the presence of the Lord and began to sing quietly:

My wonderful Lord, my wonderful Lord,
By angels and seraphs in heaven adored!
I bow at Thy shrine, my Savior divine,
*My wonderful, wonderful Lord.**

Once again, he knew that with God's help he could make it through any hard times. When he got to the office, he wrote the words and music on paper, and another song was born.

Haldor decided it might help his wife if they moved out of the crowded city to a quiet place. They found an ideal spot in the Ozark hills and bought land near the Lake of the Ozarks. Using na-

*Copyright 1938. Renewed 1966 by Lillenas Publishing Co.

tive rock, sandstone, and oak, a house was built. The huge fireplace in the living room was constructed of stones from 20 states and several countries.

The Lillenas house in the Ozarks. Haldor and his wife named it "Melody Lane."

"Since we both write music, let's call our home Melody Lane," Haldor said. Bertha Mae agreed. Many songbirds came to live in the birdhouses that Haldor built all over the property.

In 1941 Olivet Nazarene College invited Haldor to come for their graduation ceremonies. They presented him with the honorary degree of Doctor of Music.

"You are becoming famous, Haldor," Bertha Mae said with a smile.

"You are too, my dear," said Haldor. "I think the songs you have written are as well loved as mine."

Bertha Mae's health seemed to improve for a while, but in 1945, after a few weeks' illness, she died. One of her last songs was "We May Be Leaving Soon." On her tombstone, the words to another of her songs were engraved: "Jesus Took My Burden and Left Me with a Song."

Haldor sat outside his house by himself, listening to the songbirds. He missed Bertha Mae. "We lived together nearly 35 years," he said, "and I know I'll see her in heaven, but I miss her now." He walked around the property by himself, looking at the flowers and shrubs, listening to the birds sing; but nothing helped his lonely heart. Each night he sat at the grand piano in his studio, softly playing hymns, composing new songs, praying.

Then God sent a friend to Haldor by the name of Lola Kellogg. A registered nurse, she became his wife. Dr. Lillenas and his new wife spent happy years in their home in the Ozarks. They traveled to their retreat cabin in Colorado during the hot days of summer. There, Haldor enjoyed fishing in the stream and writing.

One day while Haldor was still manager of the music department of Nazarene Publishing House, a newspaper reporter came to visit them. Lola fixed a pot of tea, and the three sat by the fireplace, sipping their tea and talking.

"How many songs have you written?" asked the reporter.

"More than 3,000 songs, in over 50 songbooks," said Haldor. "It makes me happy to know that they have been translated into more than 20 different languages."

"What's your favorite song of all you've written?"

"Oh my," said Haldor, "that's a tough one." He took another sip of tea and set the cup down. "I believe it would have to be 'Wonderful Grace of Jesus.'" Then he looked out the windows, past the trees in the yard, to the far horizon. "Of course, I like 'Where They Need No Sun' and 'My Wonderful Lord.'" He laughed. "And I like 'The Garden of My Heart.' I guess I like them all."

"I understand that you are Norwegian and were born in Norway."

"Yes, I am Norwegian," said Haldor, "but I've never been back since I was a baby."

When the reporter left, Lola said, "Why don't we visit Norway, Haldor? I'd love to see the land where you were born."

Thrilled with the thought, Haldor began to plan the trip. At the age of 63, he and Lola traveled by ocean liner to Norway, visiting the island where Haldor was born and many cities in Norway.

In 1953 word came from Kansas City that a new official hymnal for the church was published. It was called *Praise and Worship* and contained 31 songs written by Haldor Lillenas.

When Haldor was 74, he had a heart attack and died in Aspen, Colorado. Many people came to his funeral.

General Superintendent Dr. G. B. Williamson preached the funeral sermon and ended it by saying, "Now this life that began in Norway was strengthened in South Dakota, inspired to lofty aspirations as he lived youthful years among the fir trees of Oregon, toughened in the long, cold winters of Minnesota, tested in the fierce trials of life's stern realities and proved under life's heavy burdens, sweetened under all circumstances, reached a climax in the mountains of Colorado, and is now victorious in 'that city where they need no sun.'"

Some said that Haldor Lillenas was the greatest gospel songwriter of his day. Others compared him to Charles Wesley, saying that Haldor Lillenas was to the Nazarenes what Wesley was to the Methodists.

When the Church of the Nazarene published another official hymnal in 1972, *Worship in Song,* it still contained 21 songs written by Haldor Lillenas.

Today, Haldor is in heaven, perhaps singing in the heavenly choir, maybe even writing some new songs to praise his wonderful Lord, and finding it true that there is holiness forevermore. As he walks with the Lord along the paths of the city where they need no sun, he may be singing one of the songs he wrote:

In the cool of the day He walks with me;
In the rose-bordered way He talks with me;
In love's holy union, And sacred communion;
*In the garden of my heart.**

*Copyright 1919. Renewed 1947 by Haldor Lillenas. Assigned to Nazarene Publishing House.

Acknowledgments

This is a story based on events in the life of Haldor Lillenas. I have tried to be as accurate as possible with dates and known information. To make the story flow, I have added dialogue and description, using many sources. Some of these are *Down Melody Lane,* Haldor's own autobiography; *The Boy with the Singing Heart,* by Grace Ramquist; *A Song Is Born,* by Bill Young; *Keep the Music Ringing,* by Fred A. Mund; *Modern Gospel Song Stories;* and the archives of the Church of the Nazarene.

Many thanks are due to Bertha Mae Lillenas' brother, Mallalieu Wilson, of Nampa, Idaho, for information that he gave me about his sister; to Gene Cutlip of Astoria, Oregon, who helped my husband and me find the old Lillenas homestead in the forest near Astoria; to Berle Henne of Point Roberts, Washington, who shared her father's story of life in a sod shanty in the early 1900s; to Dr. Earl Lee of Wrightwood, California, for an interesting conversation about Pasadena; to Oskar Fuglestad of Wenatchee, Washington, who shared his knowledge of Norway with me; and to Bob Stringfield of Lee's Summit, Missouri, who told of his years working with Haldor Lillenas.

If, in some small way, I have helped today's children know more about this great Christian musician, Haldor Lillenas, it is worth all the hours of research and writing that I have done.

—ELAINE CUNNINGHAM